A RAINBOW OF WORDS

(MORE THAN SHORT STORIES)

Suniti Kharbanda

Delhi - 110089, (India)

Edition : 2021
ISBN : 978-93-90889-05-1

A RAINBOW OF WORDS

By : Suniti Kharbanda

Price : 195/-

Cover page & Layout
Prakhar Goonj

Published by

Prakhar Goonj Publication

H-3/2, Sector - 18, Rohini, Delhi - 110089
Contact :   7982710571, 7838505899, 011-27851059
Email   :   prakhargoonj@gmail.com,
              sinha.neelu123@gmail.com

Web : https://prakhargoonjpublicationofficialwebsite.com

ACKNOWLEDGEMENTS

'**A Rainbow Of Words**' could be dreamt because of my love for the language and the habit of reading inculcated at an early life by my parents.

It came into a concrete form due to the motivation of my husband, Col Sanjay Kharbanda (Retd).

And not to be forgotten the family and family of friends who kept nudging me that publishing a book fitted my profile.

Thanks to Prakhar Goonj Publications also for publishing the book.

A BIG THANKS to all of them.

ABOUT THE AUTHOR

Suniti Kharbanda is a B. Ed. as well as a Post Graduate in Business Administration and has also been a University gold medallist. She has been associated with Educational Institutes for more than 25 years .Being married to an Army Officer she lived all over the country with her husband and picked up jobs that the new place offered. This gave her a unique distinction of having taught from KG to PG classes and to be involved in School administration. Her articles have been regularly published in newspapers like The Tribune and Daily Excelsior and magazines which include Woman's Era, Alive and Army Publications. She is an ardent Nature lover and also excels in Needle Paintings. She is now settled in Noida after the retirement of her husband.

A Rainbow Of Words, is her first book and is a collection of Short Stories interspersed with her quotations, small poems and anecdotes which add depth to her writings. The incidents, characters and settings of her book are highly relatable and carry an undertone of positivity in times of hardships. The book is sure to leave the reader a little more inclined to be happy and joyous even in face of adversities of life.

A RAINBOW OF WORDS

(MORE THAN SHORT STORIES)

™ CONTENTS

Change

It Is Through Change,
That New Things Come In My Range

❀ *The Butterfly Effect*
❀ *Bearing A Burden*

THE BUTTERFLY EFFECT

(The Butterfly Effect is a concept invented by the American meteorologist Edward N. Lorenz to highlight the possibility that small causes may have momentous effects. It is an idea which conveys that a single small incident can have a big impact in the future. The butterfly effect may take a lot of time but it eventually leads to significant outcomes.)

I was born in a middle class family as the second daughter. However my parents were very forward thinking in their outlook towards daughters as well as education. At no time did my sister and I feel that our parents would have preferred sons to daughters. We were allowed to pursue our academic studies as per our interests, without any interference. My sister, Tapasya Didi, had completed her post graduation and had appeared for State Civil Services Exams. She was not too hopeful of getting through and decided to do B.Ed. to while away the time before her 2nd attempt for the Civil Services exams. The B.Ed. application form arrived by post and was yet to be filled. Meanwhile the results of the Civil Services exams were out and Tapasya Didi had cleared it. There was celebration and joy at her sterling achievement. Since Didi no longer was going to do B.Ed., I decided to fill the form and do B.Ed. as I was already a graduate. I thought this was a light course and simultaneously I could start preparation to follow in the footsteps of my sister to join the State Administrative Services.

Filling up the unused B.Ed. form of my sister was the first flap of the butterfly wings. I studied for the B.Ed. course, loved every moment of the practice teaching which was a requirement for course completion and eventually ended up topping the course! Preparation for Administrative services took a back seat and eventually became a forgotten story! Due to my excellent performance I was offered a teaching job in the same school in which I had done my teaching practice. I was extremely elated as I felt I had found my vocation in teaching.

With the passage of time, I got married to Sankalp and also became a mother to two wonderful sons. My in-laws family was very supportive and with their help I could carry on with my teaching profession. Being constantly in the academic environment, I gravitated towards writing and co authored English Text books which could be used in schools. I was in quite a happy personal and professional space.

The second flap of butterfly wings occurred with the sad and untimely demise of the School Principal who had been my mentor and guide. The new Principal took over and there was a paradigm shift in the ways of working in the school. Slowly, all the loyalists of the previous Principal were sidelined and working in the school made uncomfortable for them. I too was in this group. At the age of 49 years I could have usefully contributed for another 11 years to my beloved school, but instead working in the school was contributing to my tensions. Going to teach in that school no longer brought the joy it had given me for the last nearly 25 years! I had always been very healthy but now frequent headaches and stomach upsets plagued me. I understood that I was very near a nervous breakdown .My caring husband was distressed at my unhappiness. He gently coaxed me to submit my resignation. I know it was the correct step if I wanted to maintain my sanity and with a heavy heart I resigned from my much loved school. There were teary eyed farewells from my students with whom I had always shared a special bond. Thus ended another chapter in my life.

I decided to take a break of an year or two before rejoining in some other school. Sankalp whisked me for a recuperative holiday to Andamans and this was the third flap of butterfly wings. The calm and serene environment, pristine beauty as well as being away from drudgery of daily routine brought calmness to my body and soul. Time seemed to be standing still as I relaxed on the beach and looked unwaveringly at the waves. The rhythmic motion of the waves was really therapeutic. I watched as the waves carried away the litter from the beach and on its return journey came laden with beautiful shells which it left behind. I wondered why the same could not happen with our thought process in life. I wished that we could sweep away the negativity and replace it with joy. Themes and thoughts seem to be churning into my mind and building up into a philosophical story. These thoughts did not let me rest until I penned them into paper as an outline of a story "Spell of the Sea". Soon it was time to leave and return back to normal life at home.

Routine activities took up a few days but the writing bug was firmly ensconced in my mind. Not working in school freed up a lot of time. My elder son was already working abroad and the younger one was in a college hostel. I completed writing the story "Spell of the Sea" and submitted it to a leading women's magazine. But, alas, my submission was met with a rejection slip. However I did not lose heart and carried out with my writings. A few of my articles started getting accepted by magazines. My creative hobby was getting an outlet and it brought me immense contentment. I still thought that my story "Spell of the Sea" was amongst my best, so I decided to edit it and make it better before resubmitting it. To my delight, this time it was accepted and was published in Eve's Era.

An ex student of mine was running a Beauty Salon

and she kept magazines for her clients to read while availing/ awaiting the beauty services. She herself had been reading my article and set it aside on the opened page when her next client came. The fourth flap of butterfly wings happened when this client, an Assistant Producer of Bollywood, came for a pedicure to the parlour and picked up the magazine as a time pass. By a stroke of my good fortune she loved my story and felt that it could be fleshed out and made into a 30 minute film for the Film Festival circuit. She convinced her Production House to think about it.

The magazine communicated to me that the Production House wanted to get in touch with me for copyrights of the story and could they share my contact details! Of course, I gave the permission and I soon enough received a call from the Production House. After a meeting with them it was decided that I would be given some amount of money and my name would also be featured in the credits of the film!

From filling up an unused B.Ed. form, working in a school, resigning from it, finding my creative hobby of writing while holidaying in Havelock beach to being a part of magical movie world, the butterfly effect had shown its enchanting results.

(Next week is the Mahurat shot of the movie and I have decided that I will attend it wearing an emerald green Saree with motifs of butterflies.)

BEARING A BURDEN

"Mom! Where are you?" shouted Kavish on returning home from school.

"Mom, listen!" chipped in his 14 year old twin Ishika.

Indira, smiled to herself in the kitchen. Her kids were always excited to share the happenings of the day with her on their return from school. It warmed her heart to be part of their roller coaster journey of life. She felt so alive and wanted in their presence. Mentally she said a quick thank you to God. She was really content with her Chartered Accountant husband, Kamal who was a caring provider, her loving son and daughter and good health of her family. Life was good.

She sat down with her children in the dining area and served them their lunch while discussing their day. It so transpired that their school was to be a venue for a District Sports Meet and those children not participating in the sports activities would be getting a 4 day holiday. Since Kavish and Ishika were not so good in sports, they would be having a long break next week.

"Mom, please call up Dad and tell him to take leave during that time and we can all go on a vacation"

"Please Mom, please!!"

"Let's wait for your Dad to come back home and we'll speak to him together." Indira knew that Kamal would be unable to say no, especially when Ishika would build a web of coaxing words.

Sure enough, in the evening, Kamal was assaulted with imploring eyes, pleading words and hopeful faces of his children. There was no option for him but to agree. Since last year's vacation was at Goa, as per the choice of Kavish, this year it had to be Ishika's choice. Her choice was a Wild Life Sanctuary. Next couple of days passed off quickly in finalizing plans, making reservations and carrying out preparations. Excitedly they set off for their holiday.

Good old fashioned accommodation, light showers, spicy pakodas and tea added charm to their stay. They were able to sight tigers, wild buffaloes, blackbucks and hordes of colourful birds. It was a rejuvenating family time for them all. On the eve of departure, Kavish and Ishika decided to go for a walk to enjoy the beautiful flowers growing profusely in that area. The flower scented air, chirping birds and animated conversations made them loose track of time. It was dusk when they realized that they should be turning back. In order to avoid scoldings from their parents for being out so late they started walking briskly and taking short cuts. In the dark they could not very clearly see their path. Kavish stepped on a snake hole and was bitten by a snake.

"Help me Ishu! I've been bitten by a snake."

"Kavu!! Be brave. Nothing will happen to you." Petrified Ishika held on to her brother, not knowing what to do but trying to give him courage. She soon found her voice and repeatedly screamed at the top of her voice "HELP, HELP."

Their parents and watchman were as it is on the lookout for the children since it was late. They heard the desperate cries of help and came running. They did whatever possible to save Kavish but it was to no avail. In the lap of nature Kavish breathed his last with his parents and twin sister close to him.

*****

Time has a way of passing, whether one likes it or not. Days turned into months and it was now six months post the tragedy. Things were so different in this household now. Joy, cheer, laughter were all a thing of the past. Each family member was besieged with guilt and sorrow. Kamal as head of the household considered himself a failure. He had been unable to protect the life of his beloved son. He repeatedly kept going over the incident and wondering what he could have done differently, so that his son would be alive today. His home reminded him too much of what he had lost. To drown his sorrow he immersed himself in his work. Socially he became morose and withdrawn.

Indira's grief was no less. Why had she not stopped her twins before they went for a walk on that fateful day? Had she done that, Kavish would be spreading his sunshine and laughter in their house as usual. Indira now became a very protective Mom to Ishika. She was now smothering her daughter with too much of possessiveness.

Ishika had lost her twin, her friend, her confidant, her playmate. It was as if a part of her had gone. Ishika and Kavish had always been the best of friends and had never felt the need of making other close friends. They had always had each other for company. Now Ishika felt herself alone to face the world. She felt that she was to blame for her brother's death. Had she not suggested Wild Life Sanctuary as a holiday destination, the mishap would never have happened. Seeing Kavu die in front of her eyes, killed something in her forever. Additionally the hormonal change of teen years, a possessive Mom, a withdrawn father who was hardly at home .....she was at breaking point.

Indira's mobile rang. It was Ishika's school coordinator calling!! She was paralyzed with fear and could not bring herself to answer the mobile. She was sure, something terrible had happened to her daughter. In all these years she had never received a call from the school. Mustering up all the reserves of courage that she had, she could just croak a whispered "Hello".

On the other end a pleasant, cultured voice enquired, "Am I speaking to Ishika's mother?" The pleasant voice gave her the confidence to answer in the affirmative.

"Ma'am, our counselor conducted a test on all the students of Class 10 today, to identify their vocational interests. We would like to talk to you about the findings of Ishika. There's nothing to worry, but I would like her father and you to come and discuss some things with us. Also Ma'am we would appreciate if Ishika's not told about this." Before terminating the call a mutually convenient time was agreed upon.

Apprehensively, Kamal and Indira reached the school. The coordinator and the counselor met them and made them feel at ease in the Meeting Room. "Sir, after conducting our tests, we realized that your daughter is exceptionally good in verbal skills and history. We counseled her to take these subjects in class 11th and discussed the career aspects with her. However she was insistent that she has to take Maths, even though she does not have much of an aptitude for it. As we chatted with her we got to know that she wants to fill the void created by Kavish's death. She feels that she has to become a Chartered Accountant, in order to help you out. She knows that you are so busy in office and hence unable to spend time at home. Had Kavish been alive he could have become a CA because he wanted to follow in his Dad's footsteps. Now that he is no longer there, Ishika feels that she has to share your office burden. If she takes subjects of her choice, she thinks that she'll be of no help to you."

Kamal and Indira were stunned to know about the whirlpool of thoughts that was going on in Ishika's mind. They had been wallowing in their own grief and guilt and had not adequately reached out to their daughter. Gently the counselor made them aware of Post Traumatic Stress Disorder (PTSD). "It could affect anyone who has endured any kind of harrowing experience. In some it leads to eating disorders, others might become socially and emotionally withdrawn, some drown in grief, yet others might take up risky behaviour (because they feel guilty about being alive). The ways of coping up in each individual is different and in Ishika's case it meant doing things which her twin would have done so that she can be your son as well as daughter."

"How do we change back our daughter to the same cheerful girl she once was?"

"Talk to her about Kavish, reassure her that the death is not her fault, go on outings like you did before, converse about trivial things and slowly the bridge of confidence and support between her and you both will be rebuilt."

Kamal and Indira understood their folly. As parents, they should have been more perceptive to the emotional needs of their daughter. They had already lost one child and could not lose the other one to the burden of expectations. With renewed determination they went back home to carry on their parental responsibility of bringing understanding, joy and cheer in the life of their beloved daughter.

Flaws —A Part Of life

When Life's Deal Seems Raw And Full Of Flaw

A Dose Of Hard Work Will Give Life A Glow

✺Kintsugi...The Golden Joinery

✺Embrace...What You Fear

KINTSUGI – THE GOLDEN JOINERY

I belong to the Army fraternity. My Dad was in the Army and so is my husband. A unique side effect of this was getting educated in many different schools all over the country…. (six to be precise) and the opportunity to revisit them and relive those childhood moments.

Last month I had gone to Lucknow and revisited my alma mater – St Paul's School. It was absolutely nostalgic to see the place where I had spent three formative years of middle school. It was a school holiday and I could at leisure move around the premises after having explained my association to the gatekeeper.

There was the assembly ground where we had tunelessly sung so many hymns, the grotto where Mother Mary lent an ear to our childish problems, and the chapel which we regularly visited before our exams. The vast playfields where we skinned our knees playing baseball and basketball were duly visited and forgotten stories associated with it remembered. The school buildings, without the hustle bustle of school children seemed strangely silent. The classrooms were locked and I could just move around the corridors reminiscing about old times. At this juncture I could also see the scratches and minor cracks in the buildings. These really jolted my mind and from it emerged a word which was lodged in my sub conscious mind…KINTSUGI. It's a Japanese word and it means Golden Joinery.

Our science teacher, Chauhan Sir was an avid traveler. After the summer holidays he would regale us with interesting tales of his travels. One such travel was to Japan and he introduced his students to the new word from Japan

Kintsugi. We were told that in Japan there is reverence for old things. The example he gave us was that when an old ceramic vase broke or developed cracks, it was joined with glue which had actual gold in it. As such the repaired vase had one or more cracks that were highlighted with gold and it became even more precious. The implication was that any flaw should not only be accepted but worked on. Only then would the repaired object become even better than the original. Similarly it is for our flaws. Once we understand our limitations and try to overcome it; we can and we will emerge as better persons. That is the Kintsugi way of life. Chauhan Sir was our class teacher in Std VII. I had a classmate Naveen who used to limp because he was Polio affected. For him the Kintsugi suggestion was that he should never be shy or diffident about walking with a limp and in fact Naveen was slowly introduced to the sport of Kho Kho where he did reasonably well.

If we look around us we will find many such Kintsugi examples like Deepa Malik, the Paralympian, who is paraplegic but has won numerous international level medals in Shot-put as well as well as Javelin throw . The late Chief Minister of Tamil Nadu—Ms Jayalalitha; she did not marry or have children, yet the masses called her Amma because she amassed love from the public and looked after them as a matriarch.Sudha Chandran lost a leg but went on to become a renowned dancer, Stephen Hawking, leading scientists of our times has no sensation below his neck…..the list is unending. Closer home all of us know of some lonely couple who have adopted pets and showered them with love or of an illiterate maid who made education of her children her focal point in life.

Kintsugi is indeed a golden concept and I thank my teacher for having enriched my life with this knowledge.

Embrace…. What You Fear

It's commonly said that
Oil and water do not mix;
But when they decided to embrace
Breathtaking rainbow patina is formed.

The eagle does not fear the storm…it awaits it
And rises on the winds that bring the storm;
And…after that…the storm loses its power
To harm the eagle.

The tiny seed is aware
That only when it's covered in dirt
With darkness all around
Will it sprout and reach the light.

When the oyster decides to embrace the irritant
A pearl may be created;
The caterpillar spins a silky cocoon around itself
And emerges as a beautiful butterfly.

By embarking and embracing a path of hard work
Mixed with awareness of failure
We can definitely reach

The pinnacle of our growth.

Difficult Circumstances

On A Negative –

You Can Always Build A Positive +

❋ The Champ

❋ Not So Good Times...Are Not So Bad Times

THE CHAMP

Aditi was an average 17 year old schoolgirl studying in a non descript town. She was a keen sportsperson who had always excelled in swimming. She had represented her school, district and had finally been selected at State level. Aditi's joy had known no bounds when she had come to Delhi for coaching at the National level. It felt as if the world was at her feet and she was born for success. To top it all she had been assigned to a young and handsome coach - Amit. The inevitable happened. Amit and Aditi were infatuated with each other. Each looked out for ways to impress the other. Aditi's swimming became more powerful as well as graceful as she vied for Amit's attention. Amit also reserved his choicest tips of swimming excellence for Aditi, so that she came to rely more and more on his advice. With Amit's help, Aditi learnt all the nitty gritty involved in excelling in her field. She soon started clocking her career best timings and even won a Bronze Medal at National level. She was ecstatic.

In this state of euphoria when Amit proposed, Aditi immediately accepted. It was like icing on the cake. That she was now 19 years and he was 33 years hardly seemed to matter to the couple in love. There was resistance from parents; but what was a love marriage without opposition! It just spurred Amit and Aditi further to tie the knot as soon as possible.

After the first flush of marriage faded, things started to get a little difficult. Aditi felt that marriage for her should bring in freedom and liberty. She wanted to go for late night parties, discos etc. She had missed all these while growing up in a small town. She understood that swimming was an integral part of life but she felt that it should not be her entire life. Amit being at a more mature age, wanted things to be stable at home. He liked to have a regular routine and a little more planning in life. He felt that these were the most productive years of their lives and should be entirely focused on winning championships. For a year this tug of war continued at home. Sometimes Aditi got her way and at other times it was Amit's will that was followed. Aditi participated in a lot of competitions but she lost more than she won. She was not giving her hundred percent to her swimming career and it showed in her performance. Amit tried to reason with her gently, affectionately and in a mature manner. It worked for some time. After some time, that technique failed and he tried arguments, scoldings and an authoritative manner. That worked for an even lesser time. Amit's frustration kept increasing. He realized that whatever Aditi and he achieved in the next 2-3 years would be the pinnacle of their career. It would go downhill after that because age would not be in Aditi's favour . He did not have any family support to help him guide Aditi. Friends were from swimming fraternity and were not a help because they were competitors.

It was then that Amit hit upon an idea. Why not use performance enhancing drugs! He discreetly checked out the various anabolic drugs. Amit believed that steroids would give Aditi a "winning edge" in developing her power, strength and increased recovery from heavy workouts. He rationalized their use by by trying to justify that using steroids caused no harm either to themselves or to others. Also, rightly or wrongly, he perceived that their competitors were also taking similar drugs, so Aditi needed to take it to compete at a similar level. He jokingly brought up the subject of using drugs with Aditi. Her reaction was an emphatic NO! Amit then decided to go for it on his own. In the guise of multivitamins and nutritional supplements, he gave his wife oral drugs. Her performance definitely got enhanced and Amit- Aditi both felt happier now that she was again winning championships more frequently. When the side effects of the drugs started, Aditi had high blood pressure, swollen ankles, nosebleeds etc. Amit started treating these side effects and also shifted to injectable drugs. He had checked that injected anabolic drugs are even more effective than oral ones and can be used for longer periods.

For some time their winning spree carried on but such things don't last long. Aditi's improved performance came under the scanner. Tests revealed her use of performance enhancing drugs. She refused to believe it. She ranted, raved and cried herself hoarse that she abhorred drugs and had never used them. Amit remained curiously silent on the issue and distanced himself from her. Aditi became a national disgrace. She went into depression and had to be hospitalized. Her parents now rallied in support of her and with their faith, love and care she slowly recovered. At the rehabilitation centre she made a deliberate effort to find out everything about drugs. Piece by piece she reconstructed the sequence of events which had led to her debacle. Much to her shock she realized that it had to be Amit who was responsible for it. She was completely shattered by this betrayal! She tried to contact him but he was always unavailable. Aditi brought the issue to the media – some believed her partially and some didn't. After all it was difficult for the media to accept the fact that she could be so naïve.

After all the negative publicity and messy divorce she had no glorious past to fall back on and no future direction in her life. She wallowed in self pity for some time but her fighting spirit soon took over. She understood that   unless she did something constructive with her life she would always be remembered for her connection with drugs only. It was then that the idea of helping sportspersons' came to her mind. What took birth was the CENTRE FOR SPORTS EXCELLENCE WITHOUT DRUGS. She put all her money into it. With Herculean effort on the part of Aditi, the sports facility slowly came into existence. The Centre had Doctors, Psychologists, Dieticians, eminent sportspersons and coaches on its panel.

Months later as she cut the ribbon for the inauguration of the centre she felt she was finally cutting a tie with her blemished past. She now had a future she could look forward to..........She had proven the world that she was indeed a CHAMP!

Not So Good Times...Are Not So Bad Times

While attending a class of Personality Development for young executives, a trick question posed to us was "Given a choice of Good Times or Bad Times, what would you choose?" We could not discuss it with the other colleagues and had to give our own answer. With our limited exposure to life our individual but unanimous choice was Good Times. The next question was "Why?" Our diverse reasons were - Feel good factor, Happiness, Ultimate aim of Life, Sense of Joy…..The trainer listened to our various answers patiently but without any comment.

We were then asked "When was the last time you made a conscious decision about inculcating a good habit and why?"

The answers ranged from, "When I had to undergo a Root Canal Treatment, I decided to brush my teeth twice a day", "I failed a job interview and decided to be always updated about current affairs", "My childhood friend was diagnosed with Diabetes and I too made a conscious decision to exercise on a more regular basis", "When my sister had an accident and was left bleeding on the road I vowed to help any accident victim I would encounter". There were mentions about poverty leading to financial prudence, death of loved ones resulting in valuing relations and making efforts towards it, failure to get into professional college and subsequently starting NGO to assist others passing through the same phase. The list was endless, but the common thread was that there was a low point in life which leads to a determination to improve the situation.

It was then that our Trainer explained to us, "The bad

times or difficult times are preparing us for better times to come. It is up to us whether we learn the right lesson from them or not". Chuckling, he added "If we do not learn, life repeats the lesson"

Now, on hindsight I realize the truth of the statement. As students, all of us have got tense before an exam and have resolved to be regular with our studies. Those of us who promptly forgot this resolve went through the same cycle, of anxiety, fear and sleepless nights before the next exams. Some students understood it the first time and kept up the resolve of regular hard work and managed to avoid the depressive phase to sail through successfully in all exams of life.

A few years back my school going niece Sampada, lamented to me, "We've got such a horrible Chemistry teacher, that I have lost all interest in the subject. I hope I am able to scrape through the subject". I chatted with her for some time and slipped in some advice without trying to be preachy (It definitely was not easy!). I told her, "Why don't you try reading the lesson in advance, so that when it is being taught in class you'll comprehend it better and can even question your Ma'am about your doubts in class. You might even enjoy seeing your teacher squirm while answering your tough questions". Something registered in her mind and she followed my advice. Soon Chemistry became interesting to her and she started excelling in it. Her teacher now did not seem quite so terrible to her. To my utmost delight she chose to graduate in Chemistry Honours and even became a University Gold Medal. Sampada epitomizes for me "Winner" after the difficult times she faced in school.

Now my blessings to the young generation is "May you occasionally have not so good times!"

Making The Best

When Stones Are Thrown At You

Use Them As Stepping Stones...Not Stopping Stones

✸ Swapping It Out

✸ Treasure Trove Of Fate

SWAPPING IT OUT

Asha and Shradha had a lot in common. Both were in their mid thirties, both were married to army officers, both had recently moved to Udhampur Cantt because of the transfer of their husbands. Their similarities did not end there. They had been given a house in the same apartment block of 16 houses and that made them practically neighbours .Their husbands had gone out for 3 months training so in effect they were single parent families being managed by the ladies. Asha had two children, Ashvi and Ahsaas, 13 and 6 years respectively. Shradha had one daughter, Shamita who was 13 years old. Ashvi and Shamita were classmates in the nearby Army school. However, this is where their similarities ended.... and that is where the problems arose.

Ashvi always felt that her mother was not smart enough. Her house and kitchen seemed to be her principal domain. Her mother was never as well dressed as Shradha Aunty. There never seemed to be any fun outings to movies and restaurants. Also Ashvi had to contribute in looking after her naughty kid brother. It seemed to her that life was not fair and that her friend Shamita was the lucky one.

Obviously Shamita was completely opposite in her thinking. She was convinced that Ashvi was the luckier girl amongst the two. Her school tiffins were so tasty, with an interesting dish every day. Her own tiffin only contained sandwiches on a daily basis. Also Asha Aunty looked like a motherly warm figure, unlike her own mom who seemed to be competing with her in the looks department. Anybody who saw Shradha and Shamita together gushingly mentioned that they seemed more like sisters rather than mother daughter. A great compliment for the mother but an annoying statement for a teenage daughter.

The complaints of these two teenagers was becoming too much for the mothers to handle. The cribbing and the comparisons seemed to be non stop. Asha Aunty made this….. or Shradha Aunty bought that!! They always felt inadequate as compared to their neighbour. They were aware that these were teenage tantrums but it was making life very unhappy for them. Also their husbands were not around to provide them support, advice and a helping hand. After nearly a month of barbed insults from their respective daughters they were near their breaking point! When they met for the first time in a Ladies Club function they started chit chatting and soon realized that they were suffering from the same problem of comparison leading to under confidence. However the confidence being reposed by their neighbour's daughter in them gave them the much needed boost in their shaky parental skills. They sat down together and hatched a plan to teach their daughters a lesson they would not forget soon. It was decided that they would be surrogate parents to their neighbour's daughter for a week! It was decided that their daughters should not be aware of this. They quietly exchanged mobile numbers so that their detailed planning could occur privately.

As per their plans, they "coincidentally" met on Saturday evening in the nearby park along with their daughters.

"Mom, she's my classmate Ashvi and her Mom! Aunty is a superb cook" Shamita said in a single breath.

"Mummy, she's Shamita and her mother," introduced Ashvi.

"Wonderful meeting you finally. I have heard so much about you Asha."

"Likewise. I was really looking forward to meeting you Shradha", playacted Asha.

"My daughter is always praising you. How she wishes that you were her Mom," said Shradha.

"Anyone would be proud to have Shamita as their child,"Asha added.

"I would have loved to be your family member", chipped in Shamita.

"And in my case, Ashvi wishes she was your daughter!"

"I would love to have Ashvi as a daughter. She seems to be so well behaved."

"It would have been so much fun had I been staying with you Aunty" chirped Ashvi elated to be praised by her friend's Mom.

Shradha and Asha simultaneously turned to their daughters as if the thought had just struck them. "This seems to be a Win - Win situation for all. Do allow Ashvi to come and stay with me for a week at least. I would love it."

"Only if you allowed Shamita to stay with me during that time".

Without giving the girls anytime to think about it and making it look as if it was the plan of their daughters, they decided to implement it from that evening itself.

The girls were asked to pack up their belongings for a week and move in with their favourite grown ups. The mothers obligingly helped them in this task. The exchange of daughters was done.

Saturday evening for Ashvi and Shradha resulted in their going for a movie and eating dinner in the Food court there. Shamita remained at home with Asha and Ahsaas playing Ludo. It was nice for Shamita to get a feeling of having a sibling. Tasty home made pizza rounded off the evening. Both girls were happy in their respective homes. The grown ups also enjoyed the peace. The next day was Sunday. Shradha let Ashvi sleep late and gave her a breakfast of oats when she got up. The day was spent lounging around in front of the TV, a visit to the parlour for manicure and pedicure, a light lunch, afternoon siesta and evening swim. For Shamita, it was different. She was woken early. Asha, Shamita and Ahsaas enjoyed a glass of homemade strawberry smoothie and then spent a couple of hours caring for their terrace garden. This was followed by delicious stuffed paranthas for breakfast. Shamita was guided to do her homework, prepare for tests in the coming week and to help Ahsaas in his school work. Sunday passed off quite fast.

The tone for the coming week had been set by the weekend. Every evening Shradha took Ashvi to some activity- Monday was Zumba class, Tuesday meant playing Basketball, Wednesday was an hour long cycling, Thursday was Yoga and Friday was devoted to a visit to the Gym. Ashvi did enjoy the activities but it left her physically drained. She had never been an active sportsperson. With all these strenuous activities, she didn't have the energy to do anything beyond homework. She was not as intelligent as Shamita and needed to spend a lot of time studying in order to do well in the class. Shradha Aunty was not focused on studies and consequently Ashvi just scraped through the class tests of that week. At the same time she missed the delicious cooking of her mother. Here she had to make do with whatever the maid cooked or by eating out. Surprisingly she missed her pesky brother a lot. Their giggles, fights, cuddling while sleeping all were fondly remembered. By Friday she was quite morose and longingly looked forward to going back home.

On the other hand, Shamita gorged on the scrumptious eats that Asha aunty made. In school she refused to share her tiffin with Ashvi, just to tease her. Initially, Shamita enjoyed bossing over little Ahsaas and loved it when he followed her around. However very soon she started getting irritated .She was not used to a sibling and thought that her private space was being invaded. Study wise she did better than before, but life seemed to be so monotonous. No outings for fun or exercise. All the tasty food and no work out had made her dull and cranky. She too couldn't wait to return home.

Early Saturday morning Ashvi and Shamita were packed and ready. Courtesy demanded that they thanked their hosts for a wonderful week and this they did. With much nostalgia and excitement they returned home and to their previous lives. Never again did they make negative comparisons against their mothers. They realized that they were unalike and that is why they required a different style of nurturing to bring out the best in them. It finally dawned on them that their mothers knew them best and had their best interests at heart.

According to the planning that they had done earlier, Shradha and Asha had playacted their roles perfectly without their daughters or foster daughters finding out! The magic of the Moms had worked! There was peace and contentment in both households.

TREASURE TROVE OF FATE

My 74 year old widowed mother was a fiercely independent woman staying on her own and managing her day to day things without taking any help from her children. We had to literally look for opportunities where we could be of some use to her. One fine day my Mom, sister and me were chatting about everything and nothing (as most mother and daughters do).She happened to mention that she had a passport but it was totally unutilized. Her wistful look pierced our hearts. My sister and I decided then and there to accompany her on a foreign holiday. We immediately started looking for alternatives…a country which was tourist friendly, had visa on arrival and food palatable to us. We homed on to Thailand as our preferred holiday destination as it met all our requirements. There was no dearth of tour operators and we finalized our departure dates for a 5 day Mother - Daughters trip.

The day ultimately dawned when we left for our "Foreign Jaunt" and my Mom's passport was finally stamped which brought a smile of fulfillment on her face. The first part of the trip included Pattaya which had the beautiful Coral island to relax in. The Alcazar show was a mesmerizing Dance performance by the "Lady boys". Also massages and fish spa helped to completely destress and relax. En route to Bangkok we could enjoy the animal world at SriRacha Tiger zoo, which has animal shows and is one of the largest zoos of the world. The Water Park and Amusement Parks in Bangkok added a fun element to the holiday. All these were some inclusive offers which were thoroughly enjoyed by us. However there was one free day in Bangkok. That unplanned day turned out to be the highlight of our trip.

On that free day, like good tourists, my Mom, my sister and I got up well in time to get an early start on the day. We took a taxi to the Golden Palace but on reaching there we got to know that there were still 2 hours before the Palace opened. We were loitering around when we struck a conversation with a Bangladeshi settled there. He guided us to go for Chao Phraya river cruise when he realized we had not done that yet. He hailed a taxi for us, conversed with the driver in the local language and sent us on our way. On reaching the pier we had many boatmen vying for our attention. We did our best to bargain but were not very successful. However our taxi driver came to our aid and got us nearly fifty percent discount. The boat ride and the floating markets were indeed a charming experience. We again reached the Golden Palace but were getting disheartened seeing the huge queues for entry. We then spoke to our present taxi driver and asked his suggestion. He told us that if we came back in 2-3 hours, the rush would have abated. Meanwhile our query was about how to pass the intervening time? The taxi driver told us that he was going to a jewelry shop XYZ to buy something for his wife's birthday. That particular shop had attractive schemes just for the day as it was their 50th establishment anniversary. He offered to take us there. Indeed it was a pleasure for us to buy a beautiful Gemstone studded bracelet for our mother at a very affordable rate. On stepping out of the shop, we thought we would lounge around in the market and do some window shopping. Strolling along we came across a quaint Buddha temple which we decided to enter. It was an old temple in need of repairs. An American art restorer was at work there and he graciously guided us around pointing out finer details of the carvings. It was indeed educational for us. By then we were all a little tired and we took our leave of our American friend. To our delight, the American insisted on seeing us off and hailed a Tuk Tuk so that we could experience authentic Thai transportation to our hotel.

By the time we reached our hotel we were physically exhausted but emotionally on a high note as on our unplanned reserve day of vacation we had actually savored the warmth and friendliness of the people around. We did not see the Golden Palace but instead filled our hearts with Golden memories. No amount of planning could have resulted in the delights we enjoyed that day.It reaffirmed our belief that when we let fate have her way she is ready to share her treasure troves.

Another Chance

When Option One Is Not Fun

There's Option Two, A Chance To Redo

✺Trrrriiinnn…Trrrriiinnn

✺You Live Only Twice

TRRRRIIINNN.....TRRRRIIINNN.....

Raghav Raj was now 66 years old. He had been working as a librarian in a small private school in Saharanpur. At the age of sixty he had officially retired from the school and he had been given a farewell. He had also been gifted an expensive watch, probably as a reminder of the 36 years he had spent in the school! Since the school had been unable to fill the post at the paltry salary they had been paying Raghav, he was given an extension 3 months at a time for nearly year and a half. However the day dawned when a suitable replacement was found and Raghav was no longer required by the school.

Raghav had been married to Sheetal, a warm and pleasant lady who had kept a happy home for him and their son. Shravan had been born quite late in their marriage, when they had nearly given up hope. He was the ray of sunshine in their lives and his smallest whim was catered to. The family savings were used for sending Shravan to good schools and Engineering College. He was quite a bright child and did well academically. Shravan fell in love with Rita who was a classmate and married her with blessings of both sets of parents. Their job requirements made them stay at Bangalore. This was closer to Rita's parents' home and slowly Shravan became more a member of his in laws house rather than his parents. He had all the luxuries there, which he had lacked in his growing up years. However his doting parents could never see any wrong in Shravan. They kept accepting his excuses of not visiting them. Their son's weekly calls home became fortnightly and that too as a formality. Raghav and Sheetal would rarely call up Shravan or Rita for fear of disturbing them in their work or socializing. Distances of the heart kept on increasing. Gradually, the only reminder of their being a family were the annual one week visit of Shravan and Rita near the Wedding Anniversary time of Raghav and Sheetal.

Post retirement, a couple of years slowly passed by. Time was not kind to Sheetal. She became bedridden with kidney problems. Hospital visits, timely medicines, dialysis, cooking and everything else that were part of running a house were a responsibility that fell on the frail and stooped shoulders of Raghav. He manfully managed it to the best of his capabilities. Luckily the medical bills were covered by insurance and he had invested some money in a private financial company which was giving him good returns. Neighbours, friends and well-wishers pitched in whenever possible. Shravan and Rita always had a litany of excuses ready about why they couldn't come just then. There were always assurances of their coming home soon to share the burden of caretaking but somehow it never materialized. Sheetal started fading in front of Raghav's eyes and ten months of ill health took its toll. One night Sheetal quietly passed on to her heavenly abode. Raghav was devastated. His son and daughter in law came to conduct the last rites but after two weeks, they went back to Bangalore to pick up the threads of their life. There was no looking back for them or the thought about how Raghav would manage all alone.

Raghav tried his best to keep busy. He went for long walks, did household works, took tuitions in the evenings and read books. All these helped in passing the time but the lonely evenings and nights were difficult. There was no one with whom he could share the ups and downs of day to day living. He had never been very social and all the social interactions had been thanks to his wife who in her quiet way had built associations. With her going away it was just books (as a true librarian) that were his constant companion. In a busy life, books had been like an oasis bringing him joy in small doses. When there was little else to keep him occupied, books were no longer as enjoyable. Failing eyesight too reduced the enjoyment of reading. Over a period of time he felt that all things that had given him happiness were no longer available to him.....Sheetal, Shravan and Rita, his job, his books..... Like the straw that finally broke the camel's back, his breaking point came when he found out that his savings in the private financial company had been lost to him as the company had disappeared overnight. A weary Raghav simply felt like leaving this world and moving on to the next one where he could again be with his beloved wife. Systematically he started preparing for it. He settled all his outstanding bills, cleaned his cupboards and house (thinking who else would do it later) and made a will leaving all his worldly possessions to his son. He made one of his infrequent calls to Shravan, spoke affectionately to him and gave him abundant blessings before finishing the call. He wrote a suicide note, being careful to convey that he was taking his own life and that no one was to be blamed. He collected the sleeping pills which had been prescribed for his wife and settled down on the bed with a glass of water. With prayers on his lips he picked up the sleeping pills. Before he could put them in his mouth, the telephone rang 'Trrrriinnn.....Trrrriiinnn".

Not wanting to leave anything unfinished, Raghav could not ignore the shrill summons. He picked up the phone and an excited voice said, "Raghav Sir, I am Mohan Giri, your student 12 years back. Do you remember me?"

Raghav remembered Mohan quite vividly….an avid reader with a bright, inquisitive mind. He had a voracious appetite for books and Raghav had indulged him by allowing him to borrow more books than he was authorized. He wondered why Mohan had called after all these years.

Mohan continued, "Sir, I have been working in Excel Steel Company and last month I was given the task of heading their Community Outreach Program."

"Congratulations beta."

"Raghav Sir, I have you to thank, for my love of reading and whatever I am today I owe it to my habit of reading and increasing my knowledge."

"So kind of you to think so Mohan beta."

"Raghav Sir, the booklover in me led me to propose starting Mobile libraries for the slums as part of the Social Outreach program. I have already received approval for it. Sir, there is some more news for you. I had gone to our school to meet you and got to know that you had retired and were not working anywhere. I forwarded your name to my company for managing these Mobile libraries and just 5 minutes back it was confirmed that it is acceptable to them. Raghav Sir if it okay with you, I will send the Company car to pick you up in half an hour and then we can start working on this project together. When you come to office, we can work out the details of your employment. I hope it is all right Raghav Sir?"

A stunned Raghav could just utter, "Yes Mohan, I will be ready in half an hour...and the project sounds just great."

Raghav flushed the sleeping pills, tore the suicide note and reflected on the miracles of God. It was really true that no good deed ever goes unrewarded if done unselfishly— Mohan had proven that. Had there been even a minute's delay in the phone call things would have been very different. He would have left this world with a "Loser's" tag. However he could now look forward to a useful and productive life, wherein by helping the slum children he would be given a new lease on life himself. With tears in his eyes but a beatific smile on his lips, he eagerly waited for Mohan's car which would lead him to the next phase of his life.

YOU LIVE ONLY TWICE

Ajay and Bindiya Deshpande were working professionals in their early thirties and were parents to a sweet tempered son, Bhavin .It was a happy and comfortable life. However there was just one thing which occasionally nibbled at their happiness and that was the absence of a daughter in the house! For three generations there had only been sons in the Deshpande family and everyone sorely missed the soft touch of a little girl. However God decided to be benevolent. They were blessed with a cute daughter when they had lost all hopes of a second child. The entire Deshpande clan was joyous and boisterous in welcoming the little angel. The hospital staff was also amazed at the lavish gifts bestowed on them at the birth of a daughter. An extravagant welcome awaited Bindiya and the little princess when they reached home. Drumbeats heralded the arrival. Balloons and streamers, rangoli and elaborate flower arrangements adorned the house. Singing, dancing and delicious food added to the gaiety. Blessings from loved ones rounded off the happiness.

Bhavin was 8 years old and had always wanted a sibling. He was secure in his family's love for him and did not display any jealousy at the attention being showered on his baby sister. The family members chose Araya, meaning princess, as the name for the little bundle of joy. Her cute looks, enchanting smile and infectious laughter lit up the house. Little Araya had all family members securely wrapped around her little finger. Her smallest wish was catered to and she was surrounded by toys, dolls and pretty clothes in addition to the love and affection.

As always happens, excess of everything brings its own problems. Surrounded by so much of love and pampering she became accustomed to having her way. She felt it was her right to be the center of everyone's life. Whenever Araya's whims were not catered to she would show peevishness and ill temper. Her parents were mature and understood that this was not the best way to bring up their daughter. They tried to bring a little discipline to her life but Araya instinctively understood which family member to manipulate for her benefit. Sometimes it was tears or tantrums and other times it was a hug, kiss or smile which acted as her weapon for victory. Since she was small her demands also were small......interesting food, delayed sleep time, another toy, more TV viewing and most of the time they succumbed to her demands.

When Araya became school going, she always had 'friends' around her. Her pretty looks, expensive accessories, unique stationery items and expensive gifts on birthdays ensured that she was never lonely. To top it all she was a gifted artist and always won Art competitions. If she had added a little hard work to her inherent intelligence she could have excelled academically too, but hard work did not really interest her.

Life carried on at an even keel. Bhavin was intelligent, hard working and focused. To the delight of his parents he secured admission in the local Medical College. He was a conscientious and diligent student and seemed eminently suitable for the profession of his choice.

Araya's 16th birthday was approaching and the family sat down together to plan for it. Ajay and Bindiya planned to have a huge bash in the 5 star Hotel near their home. They planned to call family members as well as friends of the children for a Musical Evening and dinner. Araya had plans of her own and refused to fall in with their wishes. She wanted to go to Goa with 3 of her girl friends for a week and without any adult supervision. Obviously it was not acceptable to her parents. Sulking, ill temper and tears followed to no avail. Araya shut herself in her room and refused to come out for lunch. Her parents decided that now was the time to be firm and did not budge from their stance of not giving permission. They were just finishing their Sunday lunch without Araya, when they heard a crash from their daughter's room. Rushing there, they saw Araya with a slit wrist and a shattered glass vase. She had used a sliver of glass to cut her wrist. There was blood oozing out and staining the bed sheet. Bhavin's medical training took over. He monitored his sister's pulse, cleaned up and dressed the wound. He realized the gash was not deep. It was less of a suicide attempt and more of an attention seeking act. He soothed his sister as well as pacified his parents. The next 48 hours they never left Araya alone fearing another such attempt by her. By the end of that period she was nearly fine and the other family members too had calmed down. They again sat down as a family and explained the futility of such an action to Araya. They reiterated their love for her and explained that everything could be resolved by discussion. At the end of the conversation, they agreed to go to Goa as a family for four days. Araya's 3 friends would also accompany them and in Goa the girls would be given independence to plan their daily itinerary. A truce resulted and there was a wary peace.

Things limped back to normal. Bindiya pleaded with Araya to see a counselor but Araya refused. After a couple of years when no such action was repeated by Araya, everyone rationalized her suicide attempt as a juvenile and rash act of an impulsive teenager. Araya was now in her Junior College studying Fine Arts. As often happens in college, she became infatuated by Kalpesh Sir, a young and smart teacher. She would hang on to his words, create opportunities to be near him, would put efforts in his subject so that she could be his favorite student. Kalpesh Sir understood what was happening and from his side he kept Araya at a safe distance and never singled her out for his attention. On Teachers' Day, he accepted her card and gift as she was one of the many who did that. That gave Araya a ray of hope for the future. However on Valentine's Day, when Araya gave him a card and a rose, he rebuffed her and told her it was inappropriate.

Araya was dejected .She had never tasted failure earlier. On reaching home, she pleaded a headache and secluded herself in her room. Rage, sorrow, unfulfilled love along with self pity is a hideous cocktail. Her last suicide attempt had resulted in a victory of sorts and she thought of repeating it. She wrote a note for Kalpesh Sir, conveying her undying love for him but also said that he was not to be blamed for her actions. This time she took a good dose of rat poison. By a lucky coincidence, her brother had come to her room to ask about her headache. He immediately reacted and pumped out the poison. Her parents were devastated. They went blank about the future course of action. This time it was Bhavin who decided what to do. They would admit her to a Nursing Home run by Bhavin's batch mate and friend, Dr. Chandan. Bhavin, Chandan, Ajay and Bindiya decided to try shock therapy on Araya to make her appreciate the value of life. They would be taking a risk in feeding her lies but in the hope of greater good they decided to go for it. They may earn her ire when she found out the truth, but they were willing to gamble their own future joy for Araya's happiness.

Araya was given sedatives to keep her calm for a few hours. When she regained enough strength she became aware that she was in a hospital bed. Bhavin was at her bedside with a glum expression. To her query of what happened, he did his best acting of not sharing her health report with her. On Araya's constant probing he burst into glycerin induced tears.

"Araya, we brought you to Chandan's clinic so that the whole episode could be kept discrete. Since you had ingested poison, a lot of tests were conducted. It was found out that you may possibly have a rare genetic disorder which would not allow you to live beyond 1 or 2 years. But don't lose heart. We will be carrying out a confirmatory test after a gap of 4 months. Maybe it turns out negative." He clasped her hand in his and proclaimed his brotherly love for her. He promised her that he would do everything in his capacity to heal her. He then left her alone to think about it.

Araya was shocked. She had never wanted to die. She realized that she was bestowed with more blessings than anyone she knew. She was young, pretty and talented. She belonged to a rich family and was loved dearly by her family members. She had enough friends who cared for her. She could have had a beautiful future ahead of her and she had stupidly thought of ending it prematurely! If she had limited time left, she would use it in the best possible manner and do something for her family to be proud of her. She recollected the pamphlet in college inviting entries for an upcoming All India Art Competition for freelancers. Maybe she could win that and make a mark in the field of Art. When her parents came to meet her, they could see from her behavior that she had transformed from an immature kid to a young adult. She apologized for her rash activities and told them that she was turning over a new leaf from that moment onwards. She also requested them to call Kalpesh Sir to the hospital and be present when he came. When Kalpesh Sir came, Araya apologized to him for her silly behavior. She assured him that henceforth, she would be a model student and nothing more than that. She also asked for his guidance for the forthcoming Art competition, to enable her to work towards it.

When they went back home, she showed everyone that she had a spine of steel and could work as hard as anyone else. She spent all her after college hours perfecting her techniques of drawing and painting. She did not win the All India competition but got an appreciation certificate for her unique approach to the topic. This was enough to spur her to continue her efforts. After four months, when the "medical tests" came negative for the genetic disorder, she heaved a sigh of relief. By this time she had got used to hard work and appreciation for it and did not think of reverting back to the casual lifestyle of her earlier days.

Seeing his sister as a more fulfilled individual, reminded Bhavin of the words of Ian Fleming,

"You only live twice: Once when you are born. And once when you look death in the face. "

Fitness

Being Fit

Makes Life A Hit

❀To Gym Or Not To Gym

❀Walk The Walk, Talk The Talk

TO GYM OR NOT TO GYM

I will eat, I am eating and I ate
So obviously I am overweight
And because I am not trim
I decided to join the gym
I am also over the hill
But that shouldn't prevent me using the treadmill.

In my newly bought track suit
I thought I did look cute
And in my quest to be slim
I enthusiastically hit the gym
As soon as I opened the gym door
My self confidence hit the floor.

A girl who could win a beauty title
Was on the exercise cycle
Another one using the cross trainer
Had a size zero figure
The twister enthusiast
Must be a gymnast!

I pondered about my fate
Was my slimming resolution two decades late?

A radical thought passed my mind
And so on my weight, I decided to be kind.
My thought - to make my height weight proportionate
Why not increase my height by inches six to eight?

Now I am looking for suggestions
That'll reduce my tensions
They should not be bizarre
My beauty it should not mar
But give me an hour glass figure
And make me look like a star!

WALK THE WALK, TALK THE TALK

When we cross the magical figure of fifty years of age, something happens to each one of us. We realize that we have now definitely crossed the half way mark of life even if we complete a century. In plain, simple words we are over the hill.

The same happened to me. I took stock of my life and realized that while I still had the energy, I had many things to do in my Bucket List. Keeping in mind YOLO (You Only Live Once) I started ticking off items from the list. I decided to go in with the most arduous task because after this the energy levels would be going downhill only. I zeroed down on trekking in the mountains. The next thing on the agenda was to make it an outing without the men folk, so that I could learn to manage the logistics on my own. Tour operators were shortlisted, destination chosen on basis of beauty, approachability and difficulty level of trek. The booking done was for a 3 day trek in Kangra valley. With these tasks completed; the focus was now to build up on the physical stamina. Gymming, yoga, walking, swimming and cycling started defining my everyday routines.

The day finally dawned when kitted with the trekking outfit and carrying a backpack I met with the other trekking members. The youngest member was a teenager and as the eldest in the trek, I was the Auntyji! I soon realized that it was an advantage. There was always a lot of love and respect that came my way. Realizing that at my age it was my first trek, there was always a helping hand close by. Walking through rhododendron trees, listening to the birdsong, inhaling the fragrance of wildflowers was exhilarating and rejuvenating.

On the flip side I realized that eating light food at odd timings, staying in small tents, napping in sleeping bags, using makeshift toilet arrangements, having no mobile network and no access to electricity is not for the faint hearted. But the upside was that it is this isolated environment which fosters the best of friendships because by default you spend time talking to each other rather than staring at mobile screens. Age, gender and social backgrounds become irrelevant. It is the common thread of being with each other in salubrious surroundings with adventure in your mind, which binds you together.

Though I had planned this trek in April because of the good weather, Mother Nature had other plans! The first night in the tent we were lashed with rain, hail and thunderstorms. The toilet tent flew off and had to be retrieved later! I thought that my trekking dream was doomed with the weather playing spoilsport. However the morning was bright, clear and the sun was all smiles. The trek thankfully continued. The start of the day was exciting as we crossed a shallow river with a makeshift log bridge. The freak weather ensured that there was snow in the higher reaches and we walked 10 Kms through it wearing microspikes to enable us to form a grip in the snow. Snow-bridges and glaciers that abounded were new to me and the josh was high. Drinking fresh water from the springs that criss-crossed our path replenished our sagging energy levels. The 14 km trek, half of it while gaining altitude was indeed a test of fortitude. The descent was less eventful, except that the melting snow had increased the river volumes and it was now impossible to cross as the makeshift log bridge as it had washed off! The guides were resourceful and created steps using river boulders and holding on to hands as human chains. The river crossing was now manageable.

From a sedentary lifestyle, to an action packed 3 days adventure trek, the contrast was stark but beautiful. I now understood the truth in the words of T S Eliot "Only those who will risk going too far can possibly find out how far they can go."

When the trek ended there were promises to other members that we'll be together for another trek....another mountain. Awaiting the next call from the mountains.

Loneliness And Loss

Boon Or Bane

From Loneliness, You Can Gain

❋Spell Of The Sea

❋Alone

SPELL OF THE SEA

Scene One

Balu had run away from home when he was just 12.

His parents were migrant laborers in Bihar and could barely feed their family of 7 children with their daily earnings. He was a middle child and was largely ignored. Balu's dreams of a full stomach and a permanent hut made him restless. When he heard from a neighbour's visiting relative about the ocean and its bounty of fish, he was hooked. Leaving a message with an older sibling, one fine day he just took off for the lure of the ocean. Walking, taking lifts, train journey doing odd jobs en route enabled him to reach his destination in a few months.

The moist, salty breeze, the lingering smell of fish everywhere and the early morning activity of the fishing fraternity had Balu mesmerized. Also his dream of eating well seemed possible with fish so readily available. Balu took up work with a small fisherman in return for a square meal a day. It helped Balu learn the nitty gritty of fishing and he was quite content. He was still a child and any spare time he had he spent being friends with the sea... running along the beach, swimming, building sand castles, collecting shells.

Sea activities were an endless source of joy for him. Balu was immensely happy.

Scene 2

Time elapsed. Balu was now a young adult. The

fishing community was his family now. They pestered him to get married and found him a suitable bride, who was an orphan and like him had no family ties. Balu and Chanda got married and immediately after marriage Balu took Chanda to the seaside and said "Chanda, this sea is my family and my God. Let us seek blessings from the Sea God so that our life together is joyous. May our union be blessed and our worries swept away by the sea". So saying Balu sprinkled some sea water on Chanda as a blessing from the Sea God.

Life now was even better for Balu. He had a steady income and a loving wife and home to return to after his daily toils. Their marriage was blessed with two sons Sooraj and Badal. The children also grew up loving the sea and all that it entailed.

Balu's happiness was on a high wave.

Scene 3

Sooraj was now 13 years old and helping his father on a regular basis. Whenever given an opportunity he would also take up work in the commercial boats and ships too. For a 3-4 days trip the payment used to be quite good. If the tourists included foreigners Sooraj would be able to get hefty tips too as he could use a smattering of English words and was a cheerful companion. One fine day Sooraj was working in one such ship. The compressor room developed a fault in the gas pipeline and he along with two other seamen was helping control the damage. However tragedy struck and the gas pipeline burst. The toxic fumes resulted in instantaneous death for all those present in the compressor room.

Balu and Chanda were devastated over Sooraj's death. They did not want to cry in front of their younger son Badal and would shed quiet tears at the seaside. Their salty tears mixed with the salt of the sea. There was nothing else to be done.

Scene 4

Life continued. The daily routine was a comfort in these trying times. Moneywise things were quite comfortable. There was a decent income and not much of expenditure as the sea could take care of most of their needs. Once again the family learnt to live and laugh. But fate had something else in store.

The tsunami struck and their fishing village was reduced to rubble. Balu, Chanda and Badal took refuge on top of a tree. Huge winds lashed mercilessly as they tried to cling on for dear life. They comforted each other that at least they were all together and could once again start life from scratch as Balu had done many, many years back. The branch which Balu was holding tight, snapped with his weight and the heavy gales. His last breath was in the sea which he had whole heartedly loved. He became just one more morsel which the sea had swallowed.

Balu was now in the eternal embrace of the Sea Gods.

Scene   5

Overnight Chanda and Badal had aged. All the joy and laughter had gone from their lives. It was now a monumental struggle to rebuild a life from the ruins; and it was a repeat story for almost all their neighbours. There was only shared grief all around. Food and water were scarce. The ocean was contaminated with the dead human beings and animals that had found a watery tomb due to the tsunami. Government officials warned against eating these fishes as they could be lethal. Chanda and Badal could scarcely heed this warning as they reached near starvation levels. They foraged for fishes, fruits and roots which they could cook and eat. Sometimes Chanda slept on an empty stomach so that Badal could eat. Other times Badal pretended that he had eaten so that his mother could eat a few morsels. Over a period of time the delicate stomach of the child could not digest the poisonous fish and he writhed in pain. The mother was helpless in the absence of any medical aid close by. She soothed her ailing child holding him close to her and giving him all the love she was capable of. It was to no avail. Badal succumbed to food poisoning.

Chanda once again went to the ocean front.

The entire village was witness to Chanda laughing hysterically holding forward her arms to the ocean. A kindly neighbour questioned Chanda about her action.

Chanda's reply silenced all of them "The Sea Gods have taken everyone that I loved. They have now lost all ability to harm me as I have got nothing to lose. From this moment on I have got freedom from fear."

ALONE

Alone doesn't mean lonely
It is actually quite lovely
Being away from the maddening crowd
Being by yourself
In harmony with the outer world
As well as the inner world
Being by yourself
Free and unfettered
Doing what you feel is correct
Not what others deem correct
To relax, recoup and recover
And inner strengths discover
And again face the world
With its myriad dos and don'ts.

Age In Life

Age Is Just A Number

Being Great Should Be The Endeavor

❀Live Your Life, Forget Your Age

❀My Age...I Don't Know

Live Your Life, Forget Your Age

Recently, my husband superannuated from the Army after putting in more than 34 years of service. Though we never felt the passage of the years but he was now being referred to as a veteran or a Retired officer. This forced us to rethink of our identity and slowly we started getting the feeling of being senior citizens, though we were both in our early fifties. Post retirement we decided to stay in Noida, which is a preferred destination of many retired Defence officers. Soon we started exploring the possibilities of keeping ourselves gainfully occupied. The first agenda on my husband's list was to take membership of the nearest golf course. Playing rounds of golf to his heart's delight did bring a lot of joy to him. Everyday he had anecdotes to share of his fellow golfers. What amazed me most was the fact that there were at least three golfers who were in the Ninety plus age group! Even if their eye sight was not up to the mark now, they could play reasonably well based on the layout of the course that was etched in their minds after having played for nearly three decades in that same Golf course. I mentally doffed my hat to them.

It was now my turn to enter the fitness bandwagon after having ignored it for years. I decided to take up gymming. I was aware that I would be standing out like a sore thumb amongst all the youngsters, but for the sake of my health I decided to make the effort. I joined the gym and to my surprise I realized that I need not be conscious of my age or weight as there were quite a few ladies who were in the same boat as me. I slowly started enjoying the workouts and the conversation with the fellow gymmers .By far my favourite was a white haired fit lady whose age was — 82 years! When I got to know her age I was completely floored. Over a period of time I started having regular conversations with her. The story that emerged was that she was a widow of a Defence officer. Both her sons were in service and were posted in different cities. The children were loving and affectionate and wanted their mother to stay with them, but she wanted to carry on staying in her own house till health permitted her. Along with a trusted servant and two dogs she was content in her home with her lifestyle. Every alternate day she would drive 3-4 kms to come to the gym. She had started her gym routine with her husband about 10 years ago and had decided to continue it even after the demise of her husband 3 years back. She realized that it kept her physically and mentally fit. Conversing with the fellow gymmers was part of the socializing process for her. Balance days of the week she would take walks in the community park and teach English conversation skills to the underprivileged in the same park. I am now obviously a devout follower in her band of ardent fans!!

Indeed these senior citizens are the embodiment of the words of Norman Vincent Peale, "Live your life and forget your age." Needless to say, we have embraced our retired life with renewed joy now. So many years of fulfillment of dream projects to look forward to.....

MY AGE .....
I DON'T KNOW!

You asked me.....

My age.....

I took time to ponder

But I still couldn't utter a number.

Six or seven years seems to be my mental age

When a rain puddle I deliberately splash!

I am told "You are like a teenager!"

When I stupidly don't plan for my future

Sometimes to remain twenty year old seems to be my fate

Specially when dancing merrily with old college mates

In my workplace I do ensure

That I behave fortyish and mature

When I sit down quietly engrossed in my embroidery or
knitting

To be considered near about sixty is only fitting,

On some occasions I sleep away the day

It's as if I am more than eighty and awaiting my last day.

While giving advice like a sage

Timeless seems my age.

I am all this and some more!

So for my age,

You choose a number

And to behave that age I'll try and remember.

Teaching And Learning

Always Ready To Learn, Always Ready To Teach

Makes Miracles Within Reach

✹They Serve To Teach

✹Seeds Of Learning

THEY SERVE TO TEACH

A good servant is a valuable asset. As one of my friends, Kalpana, quipped, –"When my maid comes she is greeted with a smile broader than with what I greet my husband." At my raised eyebrows she responded, "My maid decreases my work but my husband increases it!!"

Many Indians understood the luxury of having servants when they traveled abroad to their loved ones and saw them do the routine domestic tasks themselves. The balance of the privileged class of Indians have now realized the true value of servants during the Corona pandemic when they themselves did the household work without any help. However I value servants for the varied lessons that they have unknowingly taught me.

The first lesson happened nearly three decades back but it is still fresh in my mind. As a young bride I joined my husband at Dinjan in Assam in 1991. My Bengali maid Basanti was a widow. Often she would bring her 6 year old daughter, Charu, along with her so that at an early age she could start understanding the basics of household work. Basanti did her work honestly and dedicatedly and I was quite happy with her. Six months passed and it was now Durga Pooja time. The markets were flooded with clothes and other gift items. In a generous mood, I decided to buy a frock for the little child as she had a wardrobe of only 4 frocks. I chose a shiny pink frock which I thought she would like. Feeling very righteous I gifted the frock to Charu. She seemed to be happy with it and gave me a lovely smile and thanked me. I eagerly waited to see Charu wearing the gifted frock. Days passed and she had still not worn it. I could not control myself any longer and I asked her if the frock had fitted her. She replied that it had. I then enquired why she had still not worn it. "Aunty, I have 4 frocks but my cousin Lata is poor and has only two frocks. I have given it to her." Her reply stunned me. I learnt the true wealth of caring and sharing, from this little teacher of mine.

In 1999, we got transferred to Amritsar in Punjab. It was my habit that on Birthdays and Anniversaries I would distribute biscuits, vegetables or fruits in orphanage, slum area or where labourers work in construction sites. In the month of December, I went to a slum area and was distributing biscuit packets. A poor, elderly woman after accepting the packet came to me and very politely asked if I would like to have a hot cup of tea? For a moment I forgot who was giving to whom. However, on that day I understood why Punjab has always been considered a hub for warm and big hearted people.

In 2003 we took up residence in Udhampur, near Jammu. After some efforts, I could finally find a part time maid. This Dogri maid of mine was called Pinky. She was a young widow and was bringing up her son all alone. She sent him to school as she wanted him to do well in life. For that purpose she had to work extra hard. Not only was she working in 3 houses but additionally she looked after a small landholding of hers where she single handedly grew vegetables, a little maize and a little wheat. A few months later, it was winter time. One fine day, she brought a packet for me. On opening it I saw that it had about 2 Kgs of maize flour which was from her own produce. I told her that the only way I could keep it was if she accepted money for it. However she vehemently refused to take money for it. Pinky then went on to tell me that last year she had got about 15 kgs of Maize from her fields. She further narrated that out of the produce she had always offered a few maize corns to the parrots abounding there. Continuing her narration she said, "Madam, anything given with an open heart never goes waste and with the blessings of the parrots and God I have reaped more than 20 Kgs this year". She now wanted to share that bounty with me too. I was overwhelmed with the purity of her thoughts.

With such incidents abounding in my life, I realized that I was blessed that my learning was a nonstop process. Look around and I am sure you will also find teachers in unexpected people.

SEEDS OF LEARNING

Runu was baking a chocolate cake to celebrate her infant son, Apoorv turning 6 months old. Not that little Apoorv could partake of the cake, but it was just an excuse to celebrate.

Apoorv's first birthday seemed so far off that Runu decided that she would greet her husband Anand with a cake, homemade Samosas and vegetable sandwiches, when he came back home from a hard day's work at the bank.

She had just finished laying the table with fresh flowers and was dressing up Apoorv when the doorbell rang. She hastily opened the door and welcomed her husband.

Anand came in without a word and his normally observant glance missed the well laid out table and the fresh flowers. Runu realized at once that something was amiss. Was Anand unwell or had some bad news come from his/her parents.

Solicitously, she felt Anand's forehead. Thankfully no sign of fever. She then asked him, "I hope everything is all right? Why are you looking so upset?"

"My transfer orders have come. We have to go to Rasoolgarh," Anand replied desolately.

"Oh! You really had me worried. I am glad it's only a transfer order. I feared something really bad had happened. Anyway, where is Rasoolgarh and when do we have to go?"

"It is in a remote corner of Rajasthan and the place is hardly bigger than a village. I will be the only Bank

Officer there.The Officer who was posted there earlier had gone to Delhi 10 days ago. There he met with an accident and died. Since I am due for my stint of rural posting, I am being transferred there immediately. We have to leave in two weeks time."

Though the sudden death of Anand's predecessor cast a gloom on their transfer, they tried to see the brighter side of the picture as they discussed the sudden change of plans over the tea and snacks that Runu had prepared.

A rural posting had to be done sooner or later and it was better that they do it at this stage of their life. After 3 years, they would have to think about Apoorv's schooling too. Runu felt that a semi-rural environment would be good for bringing up a child. Clean air and open spaces was a rare commodity these days.

The next two weeks passed swiftly with shopping, packing and saying good byes to friends.

They reached Rasoolgarh on a hot, dusty day, after driving through dry desert areas. However Rasoolgarh itself was clean and green and they felt they would be able to settle down comfortably.

The next few days were quite hectic.Anand had to find his bearings and get the bank paperwork in a manageable state. Runu had to set up home and look after Apoorv, who was not really relishing the change in environment.

Finally, she did manage to find Gowribai, a widow to do the household work and her 10 year old daughter Ganga, to look after Apoorv.

In a month, the house was settled, the routine was

set and everything was working with clockwork precision. But Runu was dissatisfied. She had a lot of free time on her hands and nothing much to involve herself in.

She would reminisce about her previous station nostalgically. There she had been able to meet friends, go shopping, and have morning coffee sessions, go out with Anand for a movie, or chat over the phone with friends and relatives. There were books to read, recipes to exchange and even gossip. The best part was that Apoorv had company there and was happy.

Here the worst part was being cut-off from the rest of the world. Phone connectivity was poor and letters too would come just twice a week.

That reminded her… the postman had looked at her very strangely. She would definitely ask him about it the next time he came.

So, next Monday when the postman came, Runu asked him "What is the matter? Is something wrong? Do you want to say something to me?'

The postman hesitantly said, "Memsahib, if you don't mind I want to ask you something."

"Yes, go ahead."

" I read your surname, Gangopadhyay, on your letter. I wanted to ask you if you know a lady named Mukta Gangopadhyay. She must be now 55-60 years old."

"No, I don't know anybody with that name. But why do you ask?"

"18-20 years ago, when I was about 10 years old, I

was living with my drunkard father in this village itself. I would roam the streets, pick up fights, steal vegetables and fruit and while away my time."

Then a doctor came to this village. His wife's name was Mukta Gangopadhyay and she started a school in this village. That was the turning point in my life. I went to her school till class 5 and then for the next 5 years I would walk 8 kms to the nearby village to study further. That's how I did my Matric.

Then with God's grace, I managed to get this job as a postman. I owe it all to Gangopadhyay Madam. She is God for me."

Runu was deeply touched by his tale. She made up her mind that she would also do some good, so that she would also be remembered with the same reverence as the postman showed to her namesake, Mrs. Gangopadhyay.

Once determined, the opportunity was not far off.She tried to convince Gowribai about sending Ganga to school; Runu even offered to pay the fees, but Gowribai refused.

For Gowribai, Ganga was an earning member of the family. She was earning by washing clothes at 2 houses as well as looking after Apoorv. However Runu would not give up so easily.

She then took Gowribai's 8 year old son, Gokul, under her wing. Daily she would spend a couple of hours with Gokul, teaching him Hindi and English alphabet, as well as counting. She would try that Ganga be present for these sessions, so that the girl could also imbibe the basics.

Gowribai showed her appreciation by bringing the

choicest wild fruits for Runu and she taught her to make pickles and Chutneys. Within 6 months, Gokul had learnt enough to get admission in the local school. It was a very emotional day when Gokul set off for school for the very first time. He touched Runu's feet to get her blessings and had even brought her a small packet containing 4 laddoos. Runu had tears in her eyes as she embraced him and prayed for the bright future of Gokul.

Gokul would still come by occasionally for Runu's help in his studies. Her heart nearly burst with pride when he first got a "GOOD" from his teacher.

Time passed. Apoorv was now an active 18 month old toddler and both Runu and Ganga were kept on their toes looking after him. Nothing was safe any longer because he would pull down things, throw them, eat them or just play with them.

Runu also made a couple of friends in the village and with their help was learning intricate embroidery and knitting. Anand was kept busy, trying to increase the customer base for his bank.

One fine day, Runu was watering her kitchen garden and noticed that there were enough peas for making pullao. She called out to Ganga and asked her to get a basket from inside the house and to pluck the peas.

After Ganga finished the task and went inside the house to keep the peas, she heard a loud crash. She hurried inside. Apparently Apoorv finding himself unsupervised for 5 minutes, had managed to locate a bottle of toilet cleaning acid, which had been kept hidden in a corner under some woven baskets and sacks.

He was trying to open the bottle and drink it, when Ganga entered the room and read "ZEHAR" (Poison) in Hindi written in big letters. She had hurled the bottle from Apoorv's hand and that was the crash that Runu had heard.

Runu later learnt that Ganga's interest in reading had been kindled when Runu used to teach Gokul. Ganga would also read Gokul's books whenever she could and so had managed to read ZEHAR (in Hindi) just in time to save Apoorv from any harm.

Runu was overwhelmed that the seeds of learning that she had sown had borne such a rich harvest! She was now doubly determined to spread these seeds far and wide, so that the harvests would continue to get bigger and better.

Desires

We Need In Life Some Desires

To Set Life On Fire

❂Lalit, The Lapka

❂The Wish Circle

LALIT, THE LAPKA

His parents had named him Lalit, which was the name of the reigning Bollywood hero. It was a different matter that he was a scrawny tiny baby with a withered left hand. After all he was the son that they had always craved for, after begetting 3 daughters. He was the hero in the lives of his parents who were daily wage earners in Agra.

Growing up in this environment of poor, hard working parents, young dependant sisters and the great social divide between the rich tourists coming to Taj Mahal was enough to make Lalit's blood boil. Why was life so unfair? Why couldn't he and his family be comfortably off? His poverty spurred him to make something of his life. He was determined to earn money and live like a hero.

Being the hub of all foreign tourists visiting India, Agra managed to somewhat feed its multitude of poor residents due to the largesse of these visitors. Most of the foreigners could not resist the tear jerking stories of the residents and happily parted with food, money or clothing items. Poverty tourism had slowly become an industry in Agra! Lalit started making a study of foreign tourists and how he could get the better of them. The painstakingly in-depth study by observation and conversation with tourists, locals as well as guides was such, that had he written a thesis on this, it would have earned him a PhD!

By the time he was 18 years of age he had cultivated all the necessary skills to earn himself a decent living. He was always in clean and simple clothes, combed hair, neat footwear and a cultivated beguiling smile on his face. He had realized that foreigners might give alms to dirty and poor people but would not associate with them; hence the decently groomed look was important. His withered hand was always on display and earned him extra in tips. Lalit had also picked up a few basic words for conversation in English, Chinese, German, Russian and French languages because it was from these countries that the maximum footfall was in Agra. The next requirement for plying his trade was gaining acquaintance with Taxi operators, hotel managers, eateries, hospitals, policemen, pawnbrokers and various curio shopkeepers.

He had developed various modus operandi to ply his trade. If it was a British family, he took on the mantle of a tourist guide, showing them various monuments, narrating incidents of British atrocities when India was under British rule .It mattered little that the incidents were true or not! By the end of the tour the Britishers felt obliged to make up for the wrong doings of their forefathers and always handsomely tipped Lalit!

The French were even easier to handle. They loved long conversations and were generally emotionally soft targets. Lalit always had a sob story for them. His was a story of hardship and struggle that showed him as a stoic hero ready to work hard but unwilling to bow down to the miseries that came his way. Sometimes he added an angle of unrequited love, just for the sheer joy of story telling. The French readily parted with money to bring a smile to the face of this fine young man. Another facet of the French people was their fondness of good food. That too resulted in a good percentage for Lalit from the food joints where he took the French tourists.

For the young travelers, Lalit always insisted on adventurous Tonga rides, cheap curios and inexpensive dormitory stays. When he had their confidence, he along with his band of urchins managed to distract them with staged accidents or disasters and took away a carelessly kept camera, backpack or mobile phone.

For the penny pinching tourists Lalit had devised a plan in collaboration with the curio shopkeepers. He took the tourists to the shops and pretended to get a good bargain on behalf of the tourist. The shopkeeper would then indulge in small talk with the tourist and tell them that a previous tourist from their area had ordered a high quality masterpiece to be shipped to them. Since it had recently only got ready, they were about to ship it but it was a coincidence that somebody of that place had come to this shop. The shopkeeper would then show an exquisite curio to the tourist. The packet could now be delivered in his native country by hand by this tourist. He need pay only the cost of the item and could sell it to the concerned person at a hiked price. The shopkeeper convinced them that he was saving on shipping charges, so any benefit should go to the present tourist. The purchaser thought he was making a quick buck, only to realize on reaching his native place that no such addressee existed and he was stuck with a cheap replica of the masterpiece.

With his bag of tricks, scams and stories; everyday was a new opportunity of earning good money for Lalit. His parents no longer had to do bone breaking work and all his sisters were married. Life seemed to be finally comfortable for Lalit. He now started building his team of urchins by teaching them the tricks of the trade. He would get a cut from their earnings and now more areas of Agra could be covered by his group. He further fine tuned his craft and would target tourists travelling alone. His system was to catch them at airports and railway stations, the moment they set foot in Agra. His notoriety started spreading and he now had earned the title of "Lalit, the Lapka." (Lapka, literally meant jumping and catching in Hindi and that is what was being done with the tourists)

Ill earned gains are seldom lasting. The number of tourist complaints started growing and earning a bad name for the city of Taj Mahal and the tourism police had to swing into action. Using decoy customers, Lalit was caught red handed. He was sent to jail and his story hit a large number of news channels. The drama of his life caught the fancy of a Bollywood writer and soon a movie on "Lalit, the Lapka" was made.

From being named after a Bollywood star, to a movie being made on his notoriety, life had finally come a full circle!

THE WISH CIRCLE........

Every Wednesday morning the six neighbours met for coffee and snacks, turn by turn in each others homes. It was a time to sit down together and gossip about what was happening in their lives. Sometimes the lead topic was in laws, yet another day it was maid or children. Then there was the perennial favourite…shopping. There was always an element of scandalous gossip included which made them always feel better about themselves. (Thank God we are different!! And not like so and so…..)

Today they had gathered at Shama's house. She was the youngest and most vivacious amongst them. With two kids under 6 years of age, she was kept constantly on her toes. Since her husband was still in the struggling phase of his career they could not afford a full time servant and Shama would work non stop at home. Serving her guests homemade cake and sandwiches, she reflected how privileged the rest of the group members were. How she wished that she could be in the well heeled shoes of her neighbour Ravisha. Then her life could be so restful and all she had to do was to plan what she would wear for her next outing, Tiring and difficult tasks would automatically be taken care of. If only wishes could be fulfilled.....

Ravisha was an attractive lady in her 40s and was married to an Army officer. She was always well groomed and impeccably turned out. She had ample help at home and was always mentioning about attending various parties or having picnics and get-togethers. Shama wondered when her life could reach that level where she could just sit back and enjoy. Ravisha while indulging in idle chit chat had her thoughts elsewhere. How she wished that she was as professionally well settled as Vartika. With her husband's transfer every couple of years, Ravisha even with her professional qualifications had been unable to pursue a profession in which she could grow. By the time the children were admitted to their new schools, a house had been allotted, belongings unpacked and a new routine set as per the new town, a few months would have elapsed. She could just pick up jobs for the short time that they managed to stay in a particular station, but none which could challenge her or satisfy her professionally.

Ravisha's envy was Vartika, an Investment Consultant. Ravisha really desired that she was professionally doing as well as Vartika. Her office timings were 12 noon to 8:00 pm and so she could easily socialize during the mornings. She was doing exceptionally well in her career and knew the rich and powerful as they were her clients. Her generous pay packet and bonus helped her family lead a lavish lifestyle. Vartika's husband was working in an MNC and toured for at least 15 days in a month . Her 17 year old son and 15 year old daughter were on their own during the evenings. The son was doing well in school and the thought of him always brought a smile to Vartika's lips. In contrast was her daughter. She seemed to be rebelling more and more. Any amount of cajoling or scolding did not seem to help. She would spend the evenings loafing around with her friends and ignoring her studies. She was barely getting pass marks .Both Vartika and her husband were at their wits end when it came to disciplining their daughter. She wished that she could be in the paint stained boots of her friend Cherry.

Cherry was a cheerful lady in her mid thirties and had been blessed with a sunny disposition. She had an artistic temperament and a boheminian lifestyle. Her household was never spic and span. Things were carelessly strewn around but there was a lot of fun and laughter in the house. Cherry's husband was a respectable banker and their two young daughters seemed to be happy individuals. A lot of friends would keep coming and going in their apartment. There were no formalities or strict rules that were followed. Vartika was always appreciative of the fact that Cherry seemed to be a friend and confidante of her daughters, unlike the relationship of Vartika and her daughter. How she longed for the easy companionship of mother daughter. Cherry however had her own dark clouds and that were her in laws. They were of the old school of thought and would continue on their fault finding spree of their daughter in law. The initial black mark was how a struggling artist managed to entrap their hard working perfect son. The next black mark was that there was no grandson to carry on the family legacy. A third continuous matter of dissent was the careless way in which the household was run with no balanced meals and time tables adhered to. Despite their staying in a different town, they would constantly interfere through phone calls and unexpected visits. They untiringly tried to bring about a rift between their son and daughter in law, by their complaints against Cherry. So far they were unsuccessful, but the lurking fear was always there in the mind of Cherry. How Cherry wished to reach the calm stage of life in which Naina was, when in laws would be a thing of the past.

Naina was the oldest amongst the neighbours. After having lived a life with its highs and lows, she was now a calm dignified lady. She had been a homemaker all her life, supporting her Insurance Agent husband and the children. One son had completed his studies and was working abroad and the younger one had become a travel writer and was rarely home. Always used to being busy in the house with her husband and sons, Naina was now suffering from the empty nest syndrome. Her days seemed dull and meaningless. She had always wanted to work and travel the world. Money had always been an issue, so travelling was never a priority. As far as supplementing the family income went, her husband had always frowned at Naina doing that. What would everyone say if he could not meet the expenses of his family and the wife had to step out of the house to work? So Naina had lived a life which revolved around her family only. Now when she looked at her friends and neighbours, how she wished that she could be in Shama's shoes… for whom a blank canvas of life awaited. Shama could pursue her dreams and passions, travel, work, explore and make her life as meaningful as she wanted it to be. Oh! To be young again......Naina thought wistfully.

It was these wishes and the hope of fulfilling it some day that kept them all going through their lives.

May be a day would arrive when their wishes would be granted!!